Man's Approach to God

Jacques Maritain

Edited by Rene Kollar, O.S.B.

WIPF & STOCK · Eugene, Oregon

Wipf and Stock Publishers
199 W 8th Ave, Suite 3
Eugene, OR 97401

Man's Approach to God
By Maritain, Jacques and Kollar, Rene, OSB
Copyright©2011 Saint Vincent Archabbey Publications
ISBN 13: 978-1-61097-457-8
Publication date 7/1/2011

This limited edition licensed by special permission
of Saint Vincent Archabbey Publications.

Cover and interior photos: Jacques Maritain, from the University of Notre Dame Archives

Hesburgh Library, Notre Dame, IN 46556. Reprinted with permission.

Book design by Kimberley A. Opatka-Metzgar

Editorial Assistance: Brother Isidore Matthew Minerd, O.S.B.,

Sadie Stresky

Saint Vincent Archabbey Publications

Contents

Foreword

When the Benedictine monk Father Boniface Wimmer (1809-1887) arrived in New York from Rotterdam on September 16, 1846, with five students and fifteen candidates for the brotherhood, his chief goal was to educate and evangelize the German-speaking immigrants of America. After finding conditions too difficult in Carrolltown, Wimmer, a monk of the abbey of Metten in Bavaria, accepted the invitation of Bishop Michael O' Connor, the first Bishop of Pittsburgh, Pennsylvania, to settle at Saint Vincent parish, approximately forty miles east of the city, near the current day Latrobe. Wimmer arrived at the spot of his future monastery, the first Benedictine foundation in North America, on October 24, 1846. Wimmer's success was phenomenal. A college was established immediately, membership in the monastery grew, and parishes and other abbeys were founded under his direction. In 1855, Pope Pius IX elevated the community of Saint Vincent—which had grown to over 200 monks—to the status of an Abbey, and in the same year Wimmer became the first Abbot. In 1883, Pope Leo XIII bestowed on him the title of Archabbot.

Archabbot Boniface Wimmer received many recognitions and honors for his educational, missionary, and pastoral work throughout his life, and his many accomplishments are recorded in Jerome Oetgen's *An American Abbot: Boniface Wimmer, O.S.B., 1809-1887* (1997). Oetgen published another book in 2000, *Mission to America. A History of Saint Vincent Archabbey, the First Benedictine Monastery in the United States,* which chronicles the life of the monastery and Wimmer's lasting legacy. Throughout its history, the monastic community at Saint Vincent celebrated anniversaries associated with Wimmer's life in 1946, 1996, and 2009.

Archabbot Wimmer recognized the importance of education in his American monastic environment, and Oegten's books highlight his important contributions to high school, college, and seminary education. An appreciation of learning in the classical tradition and a strong dose of pragmatism formed the basis of his educational philosophy, and Wimmer articulated this approach in his much quoted statement urging teachers and students to "seek first what is necessary, then what is useful, and finally what is beautiful." To celebrate the centenary of the founding of Saint Vincent Archabbey and College in 1946, an annual lecture series was established to honor the memory of Archabbot Boniface Wimmer. In 1947, Kenneth J. Conant delivered the first Wimmer Memorial Lecture entitled *Benedictine Contributions to Church Architecture,* and the series concluded in 1970 with Paul Goodman's lecture on *Silence, Speaking, and Language.* The list of the Wimmer Memorial Lectures is printed in this publication, and those lectures which have been published by The Archabbey Press, Latrobe, Pennsylvania, are identified by an asterisk.

I have edited the published lectures given by Christopher Dawson and John Tracy Ellis, and they have been recently re-printed in a new format with an introduction or forword. The Wimmer Memorial Lecture given by Jacques Maritain in 1951, *Man's Approach to God,* was first published in 1960 by The Archabbey Press. For this new edition, Dr. Michael P. Krom, Assistant Professor of Philosophy at Saint Vincent College, wrote the introduction. My editorial changes to the 1951 publication were minor. Brother Isidore Minerd, O.S.B., of Saint Vincent Archabbey formatted this edition and offered valuable insights and suggestions.

As one can see from the list of speakers and their topics, the Wimmer Memorial Lectures still offer valuable insights into Archabbot Boniface Wimmer's approach to a Catholic, Benedictine, liberal arts education which stresses the necessary, the useful, and the beautiful as the foundation for a productive and meaningful life. Consequently, over the next several years, the Wimmer Lectures that have already been published by The Archabbey Press will appear again in a new format with an introduction, and those unpublished lectures will also be edited and published.

Rene Kollar

Introduction

Jacques Maritain (1882-1973) was one of the most influential figures in the Thomistic revival of the 20th century. Both in his personal life and in his prolific academic corpus, Maritain modeled the Church's commitment to the interrelationship between faith and reason. As John Paul II so eloquently put it, "faith and reason are like two wings on which the human spirit rises to the contemplation of truth" (Fides et Ratio, Introduction); this saying nicely summarizes Maritain's life and work.

It cannot be doubted that Maritain saw the pursuit of the Truth as a way of life and not just as an academic exercise. So seriously did he take his intellectual commitments in his student years that, along with his soon-to-be wife, Raïssa Oumansoff, he made a suicide pact that he would only break if he could find some meaning to life. Under the influence of Charles Péguy, he attended Henri Bergson's lectures and began to see the possibility of a deeper purpose that could not be captured by the scientism that dominated French intellectual culture. His willingness to follow reason wherever it may lead ultimately resulted in his conversion to Catholicism and lifelong devotion to Thomistic thought.

Maritain's works reveal an active mind capable of applying his speculative thought to virtually any subject. In general, one could say that every one of his works was an exploration of reason and its limits, and of how faith completes the natural desire to know. His 1951 Wimmer Lecture, *Man's Approach to God*, is a model specimen of this approach. While the way he addresses his topic, human "knowledge of the existence of God" *(Man's Approach to God*, 17*)*, places him squarely within the Catholic tradition, he takes seriously the Church's claim that God can be known via His creation apart from supernatural revelation. In this three-part lecture, Maritain seeks to explain how man comes to know God existentially, as well as how faith responds to and completes this search for meaning.

In the first part Maritain advances the thesis that humans are capable of coming to a pre-reflective insight into the existence of God. This requires moving behind the sciences and philosophical reasoning to "the primary reality grasped by the intellect . . . [namely] the act of existing as exercised by some visible or tangible thing" (18). Existentialism points us to this "intuition of Being" that is at the heart of all reasoning, even if reason often distorts or covers this over. This intuition of my own existence and of the existence of other things calls me out to the fact of my own death and potential for nothingness; simultaneously, however, I am aware of myself as participating in existence itself as something "completely free from nothingness and death" (20). While I am contingent and hence will die, existence itself is necessary and everlasting. Further, since "the universal whole does not exist by itself," existence is not exhausted by the universe that I encounter but is itself a participation in "Being by itself" (21), which all men call "God." This "*innocent* knowledge" of God that "has not crossed the threshold of scientific demonstration" (23) easily succumbs to false philosophy, and yet is at the foundation of the philosophical proofs for the existence of God (such as Aquinas' five ways).

In addition to this existential approach to the existence of God, Maritain takes note of two others: artistic or poetic cultivation, and moral experience. The former takes place as the artist or poet becomes aware of the source of inspiration in the desire for Beauty. While Maritain generally rejects Platonic approaches to metaphysics, this is very reminiscent of Socrates' speech in *Symposium,* where he states that through love the soul ascends from earthly things to the divine, ultimately realizing that its search for beautiful things can never be satisfied until it turns to Beauty Itself (see Plato, *Symposium,* 207b ff). Regarding moral experience, anyone who freely embraces moral goodness thereby "directs his life, without knowing it, toward the absolute Good" *(Man's Approach to God,* 25). While all three of these pre-philosophical approaches to God are valuable, the intuition of Being is most direct. Finally, implicit in this knowledge of God is the awareness that God is "absolute ontological generosity and self-subsisting love; and that such transcendent love causes, permeates, and activates every creature" (26). This awareness is where one recognizes the limits of one's own nature, for there is no conceivable way to enter into this divine love short of the Gospel revelation that God is not just to be loved, but is Love itself and that He is the bestower of His life of love on those who heed His call.

The second part of the lecture transitions to the knowledge one can have through faith. While reason can come to know God from the outside as it were, faith brings one into God's inner life and thus surpasses natural knowledge. That being said, "knowledge by faith is obscure knowledge" (27), for the truths known by faith surpass the human intellect. Thus, while the object known, God, is self-evident and supremely knowable, He is known in an imperfect mode and without the certainty that comes from philosophical knowledge. Taking up on this theme, Maritain considers the analogical nature of human knowing by way of contrast to the immediacy of faith as a grace-given insight into the Trinitarian God. When humans reason about God, they must use analogies.

Finding Being, Unity, Truth, and Beauty as the best objects of thought given their transcendental character (i.e., the fact that they "overflow any genus and category" while still "imbu[ing] each and every thing"), Maritain explains that these can be applied to God in a unique way: "The concept and names which designate perfections pertaining to the transcendental order do not vanish, do not fly into pieces, they keep their proper significance when applied to God" (30). The transcendentals are unique in that they apply more perfectly in God than they do in things, even if our mode of thinking about them is imperfect. Maritain summarizes this by saying that "to the very extent to which we know [the divine essence], it escapes our grasp, infinitely transcends our knowledge" (31).

The third and final part of this lecture brings together the insights gleaned from the previous two by discussing the extent to which human desire for God can be satisfied by faith and reason. On the one hand, reason can penetrate to the source of existence itself, yet on the other our "natural desire [for God] would be bound to remain vain" (33) were it not for faith. Thus, reason leads, perhaps not to faith, but to hope for God's self-revelation. We become aware that unless we have a capacity to receive a supernatural gift, we cannot be happy. Correspondingly, once we have faith, we realize that desire itself has also been transfigured, for "our natural desire for happiness, now become[s] desire for bliss" (33), for eternal union with God. Taking up a theme he treated in his classic work, *Scholasticism in Politics,* Maritain points out that philosophical reasoning led the ancients to an awareness of contemplation as the summit of human happiness. However, philosophical contemplation carried with it a two-fold limit: first and foremost, such activity could never take up the human person as both knower and lover but instead remained in the order of the intellect without being able to elevate the will and bodily life; secondly, it was only for the chosen few and thus consigned the many to a life without ultimate happiness. Christian contemplation is of the human person in our earthly life transfigured, and extends to all. This insight into the goodness of bodily existence and of the equal dignity of all human life is a profound source of hope that the Gospel alone can reveal to us. One might say that Maritain's lecture grew out of his desire to show that every human being, and not just philosophers, can penetrate into the depths of reality, for all bear within themselves the indelible image of God and are equally called to the communion of "love for God and love for our brothers [as] one single love of charity" (37-38).

Michael P. Krom

Wimmer Memorial Lectures

Kenneth J. Conant, "Benedictine Contributions to Church Architecture" (1947) *

Erwin Panofsky, "Gothic Architecture and Scholasticism" (1948)*

Gerald B. Phelan, "The Wisdom of Saint Anselm" (1949)*

Pitirim A. Sorokin, "The Crisis of Our Age Grows" (1950)

Jacques Maritain, "Man's Approach to God," (1951) *

William Foxwell Albright, "Towards a Theistic Humanism" (1952)*

Hugh S. Taylor, "The Catholic Intellectual in the Christian Economy" (1953)

Helen C. White, "Prayer and Poetry" (1954)*

E. A. Lowe, "The Finest Book in the World" (1955)

Stephan G. Kuttner, "Harmony from Dissonance: An Interpretation of Medieval
    Canon Law" (1956)*

Henri Maurice Peyre, "The Problem of Sincerity in Contemporary French
    Literature" (1957)

John Ching-Hsiung Wu, "Christian Influences in the Common Law" (1958)

Christopher Dawson, "The Movement Towards Christian Unity in
    the Nineteenth Century" (1960)*

Ignatius T. Eschmann, "Moral Theology Today" (1960)

Paul Oskar Kristeller, "Renaissance Philosophy and Mediaeval Tradition" (1961) *

Gerhart Burian Ladner, "Ad Imaginem Dei: The Image of Man in Mediaeval
    Art" (1962) *

Frederick D. Rossini, "Some Reflections on Science and Thermodynamics" (1963)

Jean Alfred Ladriere, "Possibility and Task of a Philosophy of Nature" (1964)

John Tracy Ellis, "A Commitment to the Truth" (1965)*

Henry Margenau, "Scientific Indeterminism and Human Freedom" (1966)*

Gunnar Myrdal, "The Problem of Objectivity in Social Research" (1967) *

Howard Mumford Jones, "History and Relevance" (1968)*

Paul Weiss, "Theology and Verification" (1969)

Paul Goodman, "Silence, Speaking, and Language" (1970)*

* Published.

Man's Approach to God

Jacques Maritain

Wimmer Memorial Lecture
1951

Wimmer Memorial Lecture

I

May I suggest, as a preliminary remark, that in order to get a sufficiently comprehensive notion of the problems which have to do with our knowledge of the existence of God, we must take into account both that approach to God which depends on the natural forces of the human mind and that approach to God which depends upon the supernatural gift of faith. Only thus can we have a complete picture of the subject.

Consequently, I shall have to complement my philosophical discussion, in this lecture, with some considerations borrowed from theology.

1. Physics is today reigning unchallenged over our minds and culture. Its progress and achievements are actually wonderful and deserve deep admiration. What is badly needed is not to disparage physics and accuse it of atomizing us, but to be aware of its very nature, its true field of knowledge and its limitations. What is badly needed is to supplement physics with another type of knowledge concerned with grasping being for its own sake. What is badly needed is a renewal of metaphysics.

No doubt there is no continuity between the world of physics and the world of metaphysics. The modern image of the atom—each day more complicated, more mysterious and more fecund in practical applications—is a mathematical image or ideal entity founded on reality, which gives us an invaluable symbolical or phenomenological knowledge of *how matter behaves*, but cannot instruct us philosophically or ontologically about *what matter is*. Yet the fact remains that the conceptions of modern science and the extraordinary progress of microphysics provide the human intellect with a scientific imagery, an imaginable or supra-imaginable picture of nature which is incomparably more favorable to the edification of a philosophy of nature and more open to the deepening labor of metaphysical reason than the old Newtonian physics. The opportunity is now given for that reconciliation between science and wisdom for which the human mind thirsts.

The *"existential"* philosophies which are today in fashion are but a sign of a certain deep want to find again the sense of Being. This want remains, however, unfulfilled, for these philosophies are still enslaved by irrationalism and seek for the revelation of existence, for ontological ecstasy, in the breaking of reason, in the experience of despair and nothingness, of anguish or absurdity. True existentialism is the work of reason.[1] It is so because the primary reality grasped by the intellect is the act of existing as exercised by some visible or tangible thing; and because it is the intuition of Being—disengaged for its own sake, and perceived at the summit of an abstractive intellection—it is the intuition of Being—even when it is distorted by the error of a system, as in Plato or Spinoza—which causes a human intellect to enter the realm of metaphysics and be capable of metaphysical intelligence.

2. From Plato and Aristotle to St. Anselm and St. Thomas Aquinas, Descartes and Leibniz, philosophers offered proofs or demonstrations of God's existence, or, as Thomas Aquinas more modestly and accurately puts it, ways of making God's existence intellectually sure—all of them are highly conceptualized and rationalized, specifically *philosophical* ways of approach. Kant criticized the proof afforded by Descartes, the so-called ontological argument, and wrongly endeavored to reduce all other ways of demonstration to this particular one, so as to envelop them in the same condemnation.[2] This was a great mistake, for the five ways pointed out by Thomas Aquinas are totally independent of the ontological argument; they hold true before any criticism and are unshakeably valid in themselves.

Yet I do not intend to consider now these highly conceptualized and rationalized, specifically *philosophical* ways of approach. When St. Paul asserted, "What is known about God is clear to them [namely, to the Gentiles], for God Himself made it clear, for since the creation of the world His invisible attributes—His everlasting power and divinity— are to be discerned and contemplated through His works,"[3] he was not only concerned with the scientifically elaborated or specifically philosophical ways of establishing God's existence, but also, and first of all, with the natural knowledge of God's existence to which the vision of created things leads the reason of any man whatsoever, be he a philosopher or not. It is this natural knowledge of God's existence that I shall consider—a knowledge which is natural not only in the sense of rational or non-supernatural, but also in the sense of *naturally* or *pre-philosophically* acquired, or prior to any philosophical, scientifically rationalized elaboration.

In other words, I submit that, before the human mind enters the sphere of perfectly formed and articulate knowledge, particularly the sphere of metaphysical knowledge, it is capable of a pre-philosophical knowledge which is *virtually metaphysical*. It is this pre-philosophical knowledge that I shall now try to outline, at least in a tentative way.[4]

3. What must be first of all stressed in this connection is, I think, the fact that, once a man is awakened to the reality of existence, once he has really perceived this tremendous fact, sometimes exhilarating, sometimes disgusting and maddening, namely, I *exist,* he is henceforth taken hold of by the intuition of Being and the implications that it involves.

Precisely speaking, this prime intuition is both the intuition of *my* existence and of the existence of things—but first and foremost of the existence of things. When it takes place, I suddenly realize that a given entity, man, mountain, or tree, exists and exercises that sovereign activity *to be* in its own way, totally self-assertive and totally implacable, completely independent from *me.* And at the same time, I realize that I also exist but as thrown back into my loneliness and frailty by such affirmation of existence in which I have positively no part, to which I am exactly as naught. So the prime intuition of Being is the intuition of the solidity and inexorability of existence; and secondly, of the death and nothingness to which *my* existence is liable. And thirdly, in the same flash of intuition, which is but my *becoming aware* of the intelligible value of Being, I realize that the solid and inexorable existence perceived in anything whatsoever implies—I don't know yet in what way, perhaps in things themselves, perhaps separately from them some absolute irrefragable existence, completely free from nothingness and death. These three intellective leaps—to actual existence as asserting itself independently from me; from this sheer objective existence to my own threatened existence; and from my existence spoiled with nothingness to absolute existence—are achieved within that same and unique intuition which philosophers would explain as the intuitive perception of the essentially analogical content of the first concept, the concept of Being.

Then—this is the second step—a quick, spontaneous reasoning, as natural as this intuition (and, as a matter of fact, more or less involved in it) immediately springs forth, as the necessary fruit of such primordial apperception and as enforced by and under its light. I see that my being, *first,* is liable to death; and second, that it depends on the totality of nature, on the universal whole whose part I am; and that Being-with-nothingness, as my own being is, implies, in order to be, Being-without-nothingness. It implies that absolute existence which I confusedly perceived as involved in my primordial intuition of existence. Now the universal whole, whose part I am, is Being-with-nothingness from the very fact that I am part of it; consequently, it does not exist by itself. And thus, finally, since the universal whole does not exist by itself, there is another, separate, whole, another Being, transcendent and self-sufficient and unknown in itself and activating all beings, which is Being-without-nothingness, that is Being by itself.

Thus the inner dynamism of the intuition of existence, or of the intelligible value of Being, causes me to see that absolute existence—or Being-without-nothingness—transcends the totality of nature, and compels me to face the existence of God.

This is not a new approach to God. It is the eternal approach of man's reason to God. What is new is the manner in which the modern mind has become aware of the simplicity and liberating power, the natural and somehow intuitive characteristics of this eternal approach. The science of the ancients was steeped in philosophy. Their scientific imagery was a pseudo-ontological imagery. Consequently, there was a kind of continuum between their knowledge of the physical world and their knowledge of God. The latter appeared as the summit of the former, a summit which was to be climbed through the manifold paths of the causal connections at play in the sublunar world and the celestial spheres. The sense of Being that ruled their universal thought was for them a too usual atmosphere to be felt as a surprising gift. At the same time, the natural intuition of existence was so strong in them that their proofs of God could take the form of the most conceptualized and rationalized scientific demonstrations, and be offered as an unrolling of logical necessities, without losing the inner energy of that intuition. Such logical machinery was quickened instinctively by the basic intuition of Being.

We are in a quite different position now. In order to solve the enigma of physical reality and to conquer the world of phenomena, our science has become a kind of Maya—a Maya which succeeds and makes us masters of nature. But the sense of Being is absent from it. Thus when we happen to experience the impact of Being upon the mind, it appears to us as a kind of intellectual revelation, and we realize clearly both its liberating and its awakening power and the fact that it involves a knowledge which is separated from that sphere of knowledge peculiar to our science. At the same time, we realize that the knowledge of God, before Being developed into logical and perfectly conceptualized demonstrations, is first and foremost a natural fruit of the intuition of existence, and forces itself upon our mind in the imperative virtue of this intuition.

In other words, we have become aware of the fact that human reason's approach to God, in its primordial reality, is neither a mere intuition, which would be suprahuman, nor is it that art-like philosophical reasoning by which it is expressed in its achieved form, each step of which is pregnant with issues and problems. Human reason's approach to God in its primordial vitality is a *natural* reasoning, that is, intuitive-like or irresistibly vitalized by, and maintained within, the intellectual flash of the intuition of existence. Then the intuition of existence, grasping in some existing reality Being-with-nothingness, makes the mind grasp by the same stroke the necessity of Being-without-nothingness. And nowhere is there any problem involved, because the illumining power of this intuition takes hold of the mind and obliges it to see. Thus it naturally proceeds in a primary intuitive flash, from imperative certainty to imperative certainty. I believe that from Descartes to Kierkegaard, the effort of modern thought—to the extent that it has not completely repudiated metaphysics, and if it its cleansed of the irrationalism which has gradually corrupted it—tends to such an awareness of the specific *naturality* of man's knowledge of God, definitely deeper than any logical process scientifically developed. It tends to the awareness of man's spontaneous knowledge of God and of the primordial and simple intuitivity in which it originates.

4. I have just tried to describe the way in which this *natural* pre-philosophical knowledge spontaneously proceeds. It implies a reasoning, but an intuitive-like reasoning, steeped in the primordial intuition of existence. I would say that this natural knowledge is a kind of *innocent* knowledge—I mean pure of any dialectics. Such knowledge involves certitude, cogent certitude, but in an imperfect logical state; it has not crossed the threshold of *scientific* demonstration, the certitude of which is critical and implies the logical overcoming of the difficulties involved; and by the same token such natural knowledge is still blissfully ignorant of these difficulties, of all that burden of objections which St. Thomas puts at the beginning of his demonstrations. Because scientific certitude and objections to be met—and the answers to the objections—come into Being together.

We see, then, that the philosophical proofs of the existence of God, say, the five ways of Thomas Aquinas, are a development and explication of this natural knowledge on the level of scientific discussion and scientific certitude. And they normally presuppose this natural knowledge, not as regards the logical structure of the demonstration, but as regards the existential condition of the thinking subject. Thus, if all the preceding observations are true, we should always—before offering the philosophical proofs, say the classical five ways[5]—make sure that those we are addressing are awakened to the primordial intuition of existence and aware of the natural knowledge of God involved in it.

Let us mention now that there are two other pre-philosophical approaches to God—namely, through art and poetry, and through moral experience.

As concerns art and poetry, suffice it to quote the famous page where Baudelaire has translated into his own language a passage from a lecture by Edgar Allan Poe on *The Poetic Principle*. It is the immortal instinct for beauty, he said,

> which makes us consider the world and its pageants as a glimpse of, a correspondence with, Heaven . . . . It is at once by poetry and *through* poetry, by music and *through* music, that the soul divines what splendors shine behind the tomb, and when an exquisite poem brings tears to the eyes, such tears are not the sign of an excess of joy, they are rather a witness of an irritated melancholy, an exigency of nerves, a nature exiled in the imperfect which would possess immediately, on this very earth, a paradise revealed.[6]

Our art, Dante said, *is the grandchild of God.* The poet completes the world of creation; he cooperates in divine balancings, he moves mysteries about; he is in natural sympathy with the secret powers that play about in the universe. A slide down the inclined plane of heaven, a push from grace: the sleeper will change sides, and will wake up with God.

In the last analysis, all genuine poetry is religious. Even if a poet has no conceptual knowledge of God, even if he is or believes he is an atheist, it is toward the primary source of Beauty that in actual fact his spiritual effort is oriented. And thus, if no intellectual or moral hindrance thwarts this spiritual dynamism, he will naturally be led by poetry to some conscious notion and awareness of the existence of that God at Whom he is unconsciously looking, in and through his art and his work.

As concerns moral experience, we may observe that when a man experiences, in a primary act of freedom, the impact of the moral good, and is thus awakened to moral existence, and directs his life toward the good for the sake of the good, then he directs his life, without knowing it, toward the absolute Good, and in this way knows God vitally, by virtue of the inner dynamism of his choice of the good, even if he does not know God in any conscious fashion or by means of any conceptual knowledge.[7] Let us suppose that no intellectual prejudice, deformation, or illusion thwarts this spiritual dynamism, and that no erroneous representation causes what is implied in the dynamism in question to be seemingly denied by conceptual thought: then the man who has really chosen the good for the sake of the good will be led by moral experience to some conscious notion and awareness of that God at Whom he is unconsciously looking in and through his primary act of freedom.

Moral experience in which man deliberating about himself chooses the moral good, *bonum honestum,* the end of his life, artistic creation which engenders in beauty, intuitive grasping of the intelligible value of the act of existing—these three approaches are existential approaches; they plunge into real existence. But the privilege of the intuition of Being is that it winds up directly in a conscious and conceptually expressed, irrefragable awareness of the existence of God.

It also carries along with itself another intuition, the intuition of the Self, of subjectivity as subjectivity, which is at the same time a discovery of the basic generosity of existence. For "it is better to give than to receive"; and that kind of spiritual existence which consists in love and the gift of oneself is the supreme revelation of existence for the Self.

But is it not impossible that the supreme cause of existence should not enjoy the supreme kind of existence? So man awakened to the sense of Being does not only know that God exists and is self-subsisting Existence, he also knows that because of this very fact God is absolute ontological generosity and self-subsisting love; and that such transcendent love causes, permeates, and activates every creature. Though human reason is helped in fact by revelation to know more perfectly these natural truths, reason is enough, the natural forces of the human mind are enough, for man to know that God is self-subsisting Love, as He is self-subsisting Intellection and self-subsisting Existence. And we also know, through the Gospel revelation, through faith, that as far as the creature is concerned, God should not only be loved but that He loves, I mean with the distinctive *madness* of love, and that there can be relations of friendship, mutual self-giving, community of life, and the sharing of a common bliss between God and His intelligent creatures: a fact which implies the supernatural order of grace and charity.

II

5. I am coming to the second part of this lecture—so we are confronted with one knowledge of God which depends solely on reason and the natural forces of the human intellect, and another knowledge of God which is knowledge by faith and deals with the supernatural order.

Knowledge by faith is obscure knowledge, knowledge in an imperfect state, because faith believes and does not see. Faith, which is a gift of God, implies the action of divine grace which innerly inspires and illumines the intellect and moves the will; it is the adherence of the intellect to truths and realities which are above the range of reason, and are believed as spoken and witnessed by the word of God, the Prime Truth itself. So the mode of knowledge by faith is imperfect, but its *object* is more valuable than anything reason can know—its object is the hidden treasure involved in the very essence of God and His own knowledge of Himself.[8]

On the contrary, knowledge of God as afforded by reason is clear and obvious knowledge, springing forth from the first intuition of Being with cogent force. Be it either merely spontaneous or philosophically elaborated, its mode is luminous, not obscure. But the object it attains is God known only as through His effects, or as the primary Cause of things can be made manifest by the very same ideas through which things are first known—God known *not* in Himself, but in the mirror of things, God in the analogical community of His Being with the being of creatures.[9]

No doubt faith also is knowledge through analogy as regards the *means* or the human *concepts* it uses. But analogy, there, does not determine the very content offered to knowledge, or the formal objectivity with which God faces the intellect, and which is the divine essence itself, the inner mystery of God as known to Himself. In faith, analogy, or rather super-analogy, deals only with the signs and means that bring such an object within our understanding.[10] To express the mystery of the Trinity, for example, it is necessary to make use of the concepts of Father, and Son, and Spirit, of generation and procession, concepts which were first supplied to us by creatures, and which God Himself uses in making Himself known to us through His Son who tells of Him, and through His Church which guards and explains the word of the Son: analogical concepts by means of which *lumen fidei,* the light of faith, reaches the inwardness of God. These concepts are the *outward silver,* as St. John of the Cross put it, by means of which we grasp the *pure gold* of divine reality.[11] Let us say, then, that faith dwells in the divine fountainhead itself, in the heart of the Increate, but that God has laid His hand over her eyes.

In contrast, merely rational and natural knowledge of God dwells in the created world, and from there gazes—without seeing it in itself—at the inaccessible source toward which all perfections of created things converge, and whose pure light natural reason can only grasp as broken in the multiplicity of those perfections. In the rational and natural knowledge of God the analogical process is the very measure and rule of knowledge. God is not attained in the name of Selfhood and incommunicable nature, or of the indivisibility of His pure and simple essence, but only to the extent that He is manifested in the reflected hues and analogical participations which things proportioned to our reason offer us. His essence is not attained as such, but only to the extent that creatures speak of it from themselves to our intellect. Thus not only is the mode of this kind of knowledge human, but its very object is proposed to the mind and constituted as the aim of knowledge only insofar as it condescends, so to speak, to human reason through the mirror of sense-perceivable things and through the analogy of Being.

6. I should like to dwell a moment on this natural knowledge of God, either spontaneous or philosophical, and to give a few indications of its analogical character.

In all things that we see and touch, there are certain objects of thought, brought out by our intellectual power of conceptual apprehension, which are called *transcendental* objects of thought, because they transcend and overflow any genus and category—they know no bounds. Such is, first of all, Being—our first object of thought. Such objects of thought as *Being, Unity, Truth, Beauty* imbue each and every thing, including the very differences through which things are distinct from each other.[12] As a result, these transcendentals, which are restricted to no thing whatever, imply in their very notion neither limitation nor imperfection; and they are ascribed to things essentially varied—to a man, to a color, to a physical energy, to a spiritual power—in an analogous, not a univocal manner. In each one of those things, they do not signify one single generic or specific nature, but something intrinsically varied, namely, a similarity in relations between similar terms; for instance: the essence of man is to his own existence as the essence of a spark of light or a melody is to its own existence.

Thus it is that such notions can be ascribed to God: Being, Truth, or Beauty are limited and imperfect *in things*, but they do not imply any limitation or imperfection *in their very notion*. They therefore can and must be ascribed to the One who is infinite and infinitely perfect—the prime cause of every being and every beauty is really Being—the very act of existing subsisting through itself—and is really true, and Truth itself, beautiful and Beauty itself.

Being, Truth, and Beauty do not imply any community of essence in the various things that exist, and are true, and are beautiful. They can therefore be ascribed to God without jeopardizing in any way the absolute and infinite difference in essence between God and the things in which we first deciphered these notions. They imply between God and things no univocal identity whatsoever, only *analogous* community.

Let us now point out that our knowledge of God—and this is true for the super-analogy of faith-knowledge as well as for the analogy of reason-knowledge—let us now point out that our knowledge of God does not only proceed through analogy. It must be added that this analogy is uncontaining, *uncircumscriptive*.[13] The concepts and names which designate perfections pertaining to the transcendental order do not vanish, do not fly into pieces, they keep their proper significance when applied to God. But although coming into effect far better in God than in things, they neither enclose nor embrace the divine reality, they leave it uncontained and uncircumscribed. *What is signified* by our analogous concepts pertains to God, and in a better way than to things. But *the manner in which we conceive them*, with the limitations it inevitably involves (since we have received those concepts from creatures), the *modus significandi* does in no way pertain to God. God is truly *ipsum esse per se subsistens*, Being itself subsisting through itself, but He does not suffer any of the circumscribing marks implied in our manner of conceiving Being, insofar as we conceive Being as distinct from Goodness, Truth, or Beauty. God exists, but He does not exist as do any of the existing things. God is good and just and merciful, God knows, God loves, but He is not good, just, or merciful, He does not know or love as any of the beings are or do which have taught us what is goodness, justice or mercy, knowledge or love. In the very degree to which they make the divine essence known to us, our concepts, while keeping their proper meaning, are absorbed into its abyss. In God, what is signified by them breaks loose—we don't know how—from *our manner of conceiving*. The divine essence is known in some fashion—and truly known—but it does not surrender itself; its own mystery remains intact, unpierced. To the very extent to which we know it, it escapes our grasp, infinitely transcends our knowledge. As St. Thomas put it after Augustine and Boethius, "Whatever form our intellect may conceive, God escapes it through His own sublimity."[14]

III

7. It is time to pass to the third and final part of this lecture. Through the natural forces of our intellect, we know that God exists, as primary Cause of things; we know God in and by His effects, but we do not know Him in and by His essence.

But it is but normal that knowing a reality—and the most important one—from the outside and by means of signs—we have a desire to know it *in itself* or to grasp it without intermediary. So we have a natural desire to *see* in His essence that very God whom we know through His creatures.[15]

Yet such a longing to know the first Cause in its essence is a longing which does not know what it is asking—like the sons of Zebedee when they asked to sit on the right and left hand of the Son of Man—because to know the first Cause in its essence—or without the medium of any other thing—means ceasing to know it through its effects, or insofar as it is Cause and first Cause; that is, ceasing to use the very way through which our intellect has come to know it and is facing it. To know the first Cause in its essence is in reality something which transcends all the forces of any created or creatable nature, it is identical with possessing the deity intuitively, in a vision in which the divine essence itself plays within our mind the part of our concepts as means of grasping intelligible objects; to know God in His essence is to know God divinely, as He is known to Himself; it is to know Him as He knows us, in His own uncreated light. To see God is supernatural, is even at the peak of the supernatural order. To see God is possible only for a divinized mind, for a mind whose subjective intellectual power is proportioned to God by that supreme participation in God's life which is called *lumen gloriae*,[16] the light of glory—for a mind whose objective intentional determination depends on nothing created, on no idea, but on the divine essence itself. Such perfect intuition is so supernatural that through it man becomes God intentionally, in the pure spirituality of this eternal intellectual act, and that through it man possesses beatitude, and enters God's very joy, an absolute happiness which, with respect to our merely natural possibilities, we could not dare to dream of.

So, when Thomas Aquinas says that if it were impossible for man to see God a natural desire would be bound to remain vain, he does not mean that the vision of God is in the natural range of our intellect; he means that the possibility for an act which is essentially supernatural must exist in man. In other words, he intends to show that there exists in our intellect a *potentia obedientialis,* a root potentiality—facing the omnipotence of God—to be divinely raised beyond all that its nature is capable of.

The longing to see God, when it is a desire which knows what it is asking, when it tends to God *as God, and as opening up His essence to the eyes of man,* is a supernatural longing rooted in supernatural faith, and distinct from the natural desire, tending to God as *first Cause*, of which I spoke a moment ago. It is grafted on this natural desire, and it also perfects and superelevates our natural desire for happiness, now become desire for bliss. But in itself, it is supernatural.

8. Thus it is that faith is a movement toward vision. Thus it is that in the dynamism of our grace-given energies, faith, which by itself can only believe but neither penetrate nor experience, demands to be vitally complemented by other supernatural virtues—the gifts of the Holy Spirit—which, thanks to the connaturality of love, make faith penetrate and experience the divine reality, and so to speak give eyes to faith—*fides oculata.*[17] For "where love is, there also are eyes." So divine contemplation is here below a token and shadow, an experienced promise of vision.

We are co-natured with God by charity. The things of God having been thus intimately joined with us, made ours, bred into our bones by the love of charity, the property of the gift of wisdom is to *make use of this love* to make it grow into an *objective means* of knowing,[18] in such a way that we not only experience our love, but it is God Himself whom we experience through our love. As John of St. Thomas puts it,

> By virtue of this union by which love adheres immediately to God, the intellect is raised by a certain affective experience to the point of judging of divine things in a higher manner than is possible for the obscurity of faith, because the intellect penetrates and knows that there is *still more* hidden substance in the things of faith than faith itself can manifest, and because it finds there *more* to love and to taste in love; and from this *more* which is hidden there, as the intellect knows through love, the intellect judges of divine things in a higher fashion, by a special instinct of the Holy Spirit.[19]

We see, then, that mystical wisdom penetrates the things of God by an experience of love which bears on that very substance which is hidden in faith. It is in the very degree to which divine reality is hidden to us—absolutely transcendent with respect to any concept or idea—that this secret wisdom experiences it. Truly Thou art a hidden God, a Savior God: all the more Saviour and Vivifier as He is hidden. The man of contemplation cherishes these dark shadows of faith, because he knows, he feels, that only in them can he intimately taste and judge by experience the depths of God. Here we are at the root of the doctrine of St. John of the Cross:

> Seek Him in faith and love, like a blind man these two guides will lead you, by roads you do not know, up to the secret of God....[20] He is hidden in you, why do you not hide yourself like Him in order to know Him and to feel Him? If a man wants to find something hidden, he must hide himself in entering its hiding place, and when he has found it he is hidden like it....[21] Always you must hold Him to be hidden, and serve Him by hiding yourself.[22]

In such an experience, the concepts are not suppressed; but all distinct concepts keep silent, they sleep, as the Apostles slept on the Mount of Olives. And the confused concepts which intervene, and which may remain wholly unperceived, play a merely accidental part. It is the connaturality of charity which plays the essential part, is the formal and decisive means of knowledge. The light of God-given contemplation is the ardor of love gleaming in the dark. That is why this supreme wisdom, this supernatural knowledge of love, is described as a giving up of knowledge and an unknowing, *a ray of darkness for the intellect*.[23] As St. Thomas puts it, quoting the Pseudo-Dionysius, "At the summit of our knowledge we know *God as unknown*."[24] *He* is known as unknown, *tamquam ignotus cognoscitur.* He is known as infinitely transcending any human or angelic knowledge; that is to say, He is known precisely *as God,* in the incomprehensible depths themselves of His deity. He is actually known—while remaining unknown and inscrutable. All particular representations have vanished away, the soul has given up everything, and given up itself. The God of faith is experienced by his reverberation, His implanting in love.

9. I have tried to explain these things at greater length in a book—*The Degrees of Knowledge*—which I beg you not to read, for the English translation is full of deadly distortions of the original meaning.[25] Now I should like to add that for the Christian philosophy of life, contemplation—I mean that supernatural contemplation of which I just spoke, and which would be better called entrance into the very states of God, of God Incarnate—is not the business of specialists or the chosen few. It is a promise to all men. Compared with the pre-Christian world, this was an astounding revolution in the *spiritual order.*

All without exception are called to the perfection of love; and that perfection cannot be attained without the radical purifications and substantial remoldings which only contemplative experience, in which man is dispossessed of himself and led by superior inspiration, can provide. As a result, this experience of divine things requests no doubt that certain men be especially dedicated to it in a uniquely contemplative state of life, but it likewise seeks to spread over the world and attract to itself all men, provided they have the will to enter the ways of the spirit, whatever their state of life may be.[26] For in whatever work they are engaged, their action can, at least as regards the *manner* in which it is done, spring from the super-abundance of contemplation, if their soul habitually makes room for the divine inspiration. Such is the teaching of the theologians from whom my philosophy likes to get its schooling.

[21] Ibid., p. 200.

[22] Ibid., p. 203.

[23] Cf. St. John of the Cross (quoting the *Pseudo-Dionysius*), *Living Flame,* str. 3, verse 3, second redaction, Silv., IV, pp. 181-183 (72-73); *Canticle,* str. 13 (14), Silv., III, p. 73.

[24] Dionysius, *Mystical Theology,* ch. 1; St. Thomas Aquinas, *In Boet. De Trinit.,* q. 1, a. 2, ad 1. *"In finem nostrae cognitionis Deum tamquam ignotum cognoscimus."*

[25] This stricture applies to distortions in the first English version. Since then Charles Scribner and Sons have published a new and trustworthy translation.

[26] Cf. R. Garrigou-Lagrange, *Perfection Chrétienne et Contemplation;* Jacques et Raïssa Maritain, *De la Vie d'Oraison,* new edition, Paris, Rouart, 1947, Note IV.

[27] Cf. my essay "Action and Contemplation" in *Scholasticism and Politics,* New York, Macmillan, 1940.

[28] Cf. R. Voillaume, *Au Coeur des masses (La Vie religieuse des Petits Frères du Père de Foucauld).* Paris, éd. du Cerf, 1950.

29790449R00024

Made in the USA
Columbia, SC
24 October 2018